Bushi-Jutsu

The Science of
the Warrior

By
Andy Paskin & Darren Westwood

Published by BJR Publishing

Published by: BJR Publishing, PO Box 3887, Tipton DY4 8WP, UK.

Published in association with: Summersdale Publishers Ltd, 46 West Street, Chichester, West Sussex PO19 1RP, United Kingdom. www.summersdale.com.

Cover illustration by: Ian Turner 2002.

Photography by: Michelle Westwood 2004.

Typesetting and cover by: My Word!, 138 Railway Terrace, Rugby, Warwickshire CV21 3HN.

Printed and bound in Great Britain by Bookcraft (Bath) Ltd, Midsomer Norton, Somerset.

A CIP Catalogue record for this book is available from the British Library.

ISBN: 0 9547364 0 0

Important note:

The authors, publishers and distributors of this book accept no responsibility for any prosecutions, proceedings or litigation brought or instituted against any person or body as a result of the use or misuse of the information or any techniques described in this book or any loss, injury or damage caused thereby.

Some of the techniques described in this book require high levels of skill and physical fitness.

The techniques described herein must only be practised by those in good health and under qualified supervision.

Warning

The techniques and descriptions contained herein can be extremely dangerous or even fatal and must not be attempted by anyone who is not under expert supervision.

This book is not recommended for non-martial artists or ANYONE under the age of 18 – any person using or attempting to use any of the information from this book do so entirely at their own risk.

The sole intent of this book is to act as a training aid to the reader to supplement training received from a qualified coach in the performance, interpretation and application of Kata.

All readers should be aware of, and adhere to, all appropriate law and legislation relating to self-defence.

Dedication

For my family for their unwavering support.
For my wife for putting up with my constant study.
For my son who is always my gerbil (or is it guinea pig?).
For our students who are a constant source of wonder.
For my Nan who always protected and watched out for me.
For my Mom who continues to fight hard everyday and from whom I inherited my stubborn streak.
Particularly for my Dad whose strength of character and force of will, right to the very end, will inspire me evermore.
We've been through some tough times together.
Thank you all for being there.

Daz (December 2003)

For my family for all their help and solid support over the last couple of years – I don't know what I would've done without you all.
God bless all of ya.
For my Brother who was also my best mate who sadly died in August 2000 at the young age of 37.
Last, but not least, for my Mother who, to me, was a fighter in her own right – the bravest person I have ever known.
She fought for two years with no complaints.
If it wasn't for her, I wouldn't be the man I am today.
God bless ya Mom and God bless ya John.

Andy (December 2003)

Foreword

In recent years we have seen a resurgence of interest in the original purpose of the martial arts (effective self-protection). As a result, a growing proportion of martial artists are no longer content to practice their chosen art simply as a form of exercise, a means of character development or as a sport. As worthwhile as those aspects of martial training may be, a rapidly growing number of students also wish to ensure that their training will adequately prepare them for live situations should the worst happen. Effective self-protection and combative skills were what the martial arts were originally created for. However, if we are honest, we have to admit that the training in many modern Dojos is found wanting in this regard.

Anyone who has been in, or has seen a real fight will know that real situations are frantic and chaotic affairs. It can be difficult to see how the rigidity and formality of most modern training can be applied in the chaos of live confrontation? An observer to such a confrontation will also notice how there is no interchange of 'compatible techniques', neither do the combatants stay at a single range. Instead, we see the frenzied flailing of limbs and ranges being lost in a split-second.

Modern Karate practise tends to only concern itself with mid- to long-range formally executed Karate-style attacks. There is little in the way of close-range techniques or methodologies. We see no grabbing, no close-range striking, no ground-work etc. We only see compatible techniques at a fixed range. In short, we see no chaos!

It can be difficult to comprehend how modern Karate – which is, after all, said to be specifically designed for self-protection – can be applied when removed from the structured and precise world of the Dojo. So how do we ensure that our art fulfils its original purpose and returns to being a valid and functional combative system? The great irony and perceived paradox is that the answer is found in arguably the most structured and precise part of Karate training: the Kata!

The Kata are essentially a record of the original Karate system; a system which was designed to deal with the chaotic nature of a live confrontation. Within the Kata we can find all the skills and methods we need for live combat, providing we know how and where to look. The Kata contains punches, kicks, close-range strikes, chokes, holds, takedowns, strangles etc. We simply need to be able to access that 'lost' information and reintroduce it into our training. This is where this very informative book by Andy Paskin and Darren Westwood will be of help.

This book is written in a warm and engaging matter that will make this fascinating subject easily accessible to all. Not only do Andy and Darren share their interpretation of the three of the 'basic' Katas, but they also cover such subjects as effective power generation, kneeing, head-butting, locks, chokes, strangles and some ways to realistically apply the 'blocking' techniques of the forms. It is this kind of knowledge that is needed if we are to ensure that Karate is practised as a pragmatic and effective system.

As interest in the practical application of the forms (Bunkai) grows, it is vitally important that we Karateka with a pragmatic-bias share our information, views, opinions and preferences as widely as possible. This will ensure that those who wish to practise the art of Karate, in its most complete form, are free to do so in a way that works for them as individuals. Darren and Andy are to be congratulated for making their approach to the practical application of Kata techniques available to all in what I'm sure will be the first of many books. I'm certain that this very accessible book will be warmly welcomed by the thinking Karateka and all those looking to find meaning in their Kata.

Iain Abernethy 2004

Contents

Introduction

The decision to write this book was one which was taken following careful consideration.

A number of students have, in the near and distant past, requested a book be written which covers all of the aspects of Kata Bunkai (or Bunkai-Jutsu) as a 'take-home sensei' and this is the result of those requests.

The *reason* for writing the book is another story entirely.

We have, as all good Karateka should, studied our art extensively, both from a practical and academic point of view and, during the course of those studies, have encountered a certain 'Kata Mythology'.

This mythology is prevalent throughout *modern* Karate and this, coupled with a number of other incidents, led us down this narrative route.

A typical mindset of this type of thinking is below, in italics:

'The Kata are a set of prearranged movements whereby the Karateka engages in battle with imaginary opponents. Kata contains all of the techniques and principles of Karate and, after practising each literally thousands of times, the movements become automatic and instinctive.

This will enable the Karateka to defend against and attack many opponents at once.

Kata is meant to train the mind, and is not intended only for conceptual and intellectual self-defence. Its real purpose is to bring it in contact with the real self. Kata, in the traditional sense, is a spiritual ritual. The essence of the art of Karate is attaining a spiritual goal through the practice of the Kata, so that the Karateka competes against himself and succeeds in conquering himself.

The basis of Kata lies in the concept 'Karate ni sente nashi', which is translated as 'in Karate, one does not make the first move.' All Kata begin with defence and end with defence. The Kata teaches that the true Karateka never strikes first, and never strikes in anger.

Now, we have been accused in the past of being too forthright in our analysis of certain subjects, but we would ask, 'Can you be TOO forthright?'

We think not and, with this in mind, the example above, in its fundamental analysis of Kata, is incorrect.

Visualisation is certainly as important an aspect of Karate as is posturing and body shifting but is certainly not the basis of Kata.

Equally, Kata does contain techniques and principles within it but this, alone cannot sufficiently define Kata.

Kata is the spirit, true meaning and purpose of Karate.

ALL Karate is found within Kata.

As for multiple attackers – the best defence is to run away....quickly!

The 'spiritual ritual' aspect of Kata is fine as a consideration but the reality of Kata is that it will enable the Karateka to deliver devastating technique to any would-be assailant.

In Kata, there is NO preparatory movement, there is NO stylised posturing, NO showboating and, perhaps most controversially of all, there is NO purely defensive technique.

All of the technique(s) within a Kata are offensive (in the sense that they intercept an attack rather than defend against it) and all use projection and 'soft' techniques in approximately equal measure.

Likewise, each and every technique within a Kata has a Kakushi Waza (Hidden Technique) which, when analysed and understood is, in fact, quite frightening in its brutality but, as we all should remember, these techniques were developed for only one thing....combat!

The Kata certainly does NOT teach that the Karateka never strikes first; in fact, it teaches that the true Karateka will not instigate combat but, when a combatant launches a strike, the Karateka will either intercept or will pre-empt, that is to say, out-pace, his assailant and will, indeed, strike first!

We will, however, concede that you should never strike in anger.

Within this book you will find:

Oyo	the various application(s) of the technique
Henka	the variation and change developed from the technique
Kakushi Waza	the hidden technique

We will concentrate on the Kata which is considered 'lower-level' although we hope to prove that even the humble Kihon, when fully analysed, is an insight of devastating effectiveness of this, our beloved Karate.

Read on!

1.0 – The Authors

Sensei A Paskin (Left):

Sensei Paskin has been training for some 20 years in various forms of martial arts, though predominantly Karate.

Shotokan Karate established the initial interest.

A period of study around the boxing arts came next.

Sensei Paskin then shifted to Shorin-Ryu, which he believed was closer to the roots of true Karate.

Finally, Sensei Paskin's life-long study of the martial sciences has led to (and continues to develop) a study of Bushi-Jutsu – Warrior Science.

Sensei D Westwood (Right):

Sensei Westwood has trained for approximately the same amount of time as Sensei Paskin. However, his roots spring from Wado-Ryu Karate.

In addition, Sensei Westwood has also studied Ju-Jutsu and Chinese Gong-Fu.

Like Sensei Paskin, Sensei Westwood now devotes all of his time to the study of Bushi-Jutsu – Warrior Science.

Both have had some 'live' experience but this was during the energetic exchanges experienced during the hormone-fuelled periods of adolescence and early adulthood.

2.0 – Karate & Kata

It is important, in our opinion, to understand the associated history of the Kata contained within this book as, without this, your appreciation of the Kata, their intrinsic development and their historical significance will be impeded.

Access to the Kakushi Waza of the Kata has been deliberately veiled.

Probably, in their original form, the Kata were much more deliberate in their communication of technique. However, following the introduction of certain Kata into the education curriculum, they were 'watered down' in order to conceal the brutality of certain techniques.

These watered down versions are now practised, throughout the Karate world (with certain obvious exceptions) as 'traditional forms'.

Some instructors will, in our experience, not teach Bunkai in any form (DW was never taught Bunkai and AP was taught that it was a defence against (or within) a mass brawl!!).

Others will dictate Bunkai and others still will be prepared to discuss Kata application providing their opinions are not too closely scrutinised.

We would suggest that if your current Sensei falls into any of the above categories, you might want to try a different ryu!

Kata Bunkai, inside a Dojo, should be studied.

All Kihon Ippon and all Ippon Kumite (and Kumite in general, as practised) should consider the technique(s) of Kata.

Too much emphasis these days is placed on mass tutoring within a ryu, with very little time allowed for one-to-one tuition, and this is where the real understanding and communication of Bunkai will take place.

Certainly our students, when developing Kihon Ippons for gradings, are encouraged to look to the Kata of their grade for inspiration.

It's a good starting point.

Furthermore, Karate, in general terms, is thought of as a kicking and punching system.

In our opinion, nothing could be further from the reality.

Our lower grades are encouraged to block and counter but not in isolation of grappling and close-quarter combat considerations.

You will be very lucky indeed if your confrontations, thus far, have enabled you to remain standing whilst incapacitating your opponent.

Almost all fights will enter a 'grappling stage' at some point and many will go to ground – being able to do a spinning jumping reverse roundhouse kick, when someone has you by the throat on the floor of the local night club, will not help you a great deal!

The reality of combat is that you may be exposed to extremes of violence in a confrontational situation and you should be prepared to fight fire with fire.

Should you be attacked for your wallet, your mobile phone, your jewellery or just because someone has taken a disliking to you, you should be prepared to be exposed to this extreme violence.

At this point, you will either choose (if I can paraphrase the great combat tactician, Geoff Thompson) fight or flight.

Again, the reality is that flight may be impossible and you will be forced to subsequently choose aggression or submission – to retaliate or to be the victim.

Undoubtedly, there will be occasions when strikes (whether punches or kicks) will not succeed in concluding a confrontation – a fact for which most Karateka are woefully ill prepared.

When the 'one puncher' fails, the situation will inevitably go close quarter.

The techniques contained within this book, we hope, will prepare you for the worst kind of violent confrontation and enable you to retaliate with devastating effect!

It should be noted, however, that the employment of some of the techniques we will describe may have serious, or even fatal, consequences and, therefore, should ONLY BE USED IN A LIFE-THREATENING OR EXTREMELY HIGH-RISK SITUATION!

The choice to include these techniques within this book was one which followed careful consideration.

The reason for choosing to do so stems from the fact that we believe that the original intent of the techniques was the 'lethal force' we refer to.

The masters of old did not want an aggressor returning again and again.

They wanted the first confrontation to be the only confrontation.

Likewise, they would not be so unrealistic as to think that a hand-to-hand fight could be ended with a single blow (without prevailing luck or a very high degree of skill).

Now, we may be living in a totally different cultural society and environment and we may be hundreds of years past the time when these Kata were developed, but we believe that the essence of combat (and the predictability of such) has remained unchanged these many centuries.

The thrust of the message here is EXERCISE EXTREME CAUTION!

We would now encourage you to ask yourself a question.

Do you believe that your Sensei is a veteran warrior who has seen a lot of action in real combat situations?

We would hope not as the essence of Karate is that it is taught to enable you to NOT HAVE TO FIGHT.

There are, however, certain advantages to having been exposed to aggression in real-life situations.

One of these advantages is the ability to predict what would be effective 'on the street'.

Both DW and AP have some 'street' experience (see the passage on the Authors) and, many times in the Dojo whilst studying Bunkai, been forced to concede that some technique which the Karate world consider 'effective' would have little or no value in a 'real' fight.

We would encourage you to read 'Watch My Back' by Geoff Thompson, a gritty, realistic and brutal insight into the world of 'Street Fighting' – Real Combat!

Also, *Bunkai Jutsu* and *Karate's Grappling Methods* by Iain Abernethy will also prepare you for the brutal reality!

In our experience, the Karate-Do Karateka will tell you that 'this is a block and this is a punch and it is from Kihon Kata' – this is the way of Karate.

The Karate-Jitsu Karateka will tell you a little more of the intricacy of the technique but from a stylised perspective – this is the Art of Karate.

We, the Karate-Jutsu Karateka, will tell you that it doesn't matter whether you look good or not, that if a 'block' can be used as a strike, do it, that if you need to bite, gouge, strike the throat or squeeze the testicles to win the fight, do it – this is the Science of Karate.

Within this book, we will show the Way, the Art and the Science.

We do not wish to emphasise or over-emphasise any aspect of interpretation.

The classical is just as important to the development of the individual as the contemporary and brutal reality.

Within Oyo, we have attempted to show the classical application of Bunkai as it is taught in most contemporary Dojo today.

Within the Henka, we have attempted to show the stylised variation of application with a little more emphasis on effect.

Within Kakushi Waza, we have attempted to show the reality of Bunkai – that which the Kata was created to communicate and which is the most effective of the three types we have chosen to include.

You will probably note that, during some of the sequences, there is still the push and pull motion common to the striking arts.

This is generally still observed for balance of the technique and provides a position to fire a strike if necessary should a technique fail in its application – yes....it does happen!

3.0 – Kata History and Style Genealogy

A s previously stated, we place a lot of emphasis and importance on the understanding and appreciation of Kata history and the background of your style.

Obviously, you will need to study this yourself as, if we tried to include it all in this book, we would perhaps have the War & Peace of Bunkai here!

Emulation is obviously the means by which students learn, develop and perfect their technique but, have we considered why these techniques have been 'hidden' in Kata?

In the previous section, we mentioned the 'watering down' of Kata to allow teaching in school. However, the chronicling of data through physical motion is timeless.

Ancient philosophies tended to include the use of stylised 'dancing' as a means with which to equip future generations with this cultural knowledge.

An obvious inclusion in this cultural communication is the ability to battle and, perhaps in feudal Japan, the need to conceal this knowledge resulted in the first Kata coming into being.

Sometime around the 11th century, during the wartime period, an incursion of Japanese warriors (Samurai) on the island of Okinawa meant an influx of additional martial knowledge which was previously not a part of the norm had been taken place.

Around the end of the 14th century, a Chinese incursion on the island further developed what was already a formidable fighting system.

A direct result of this would have been the influence of Chinese culture within the predominantly Japanese combat ethos.

Those of you who have also studied the Chinese arts properly will have an inkling of the type of influence this will have had.

If your knowledge of the history of Kata is poor, allow us to tell you a little about Shurite, Nahate and Tomarite in the form of the following development matrix:

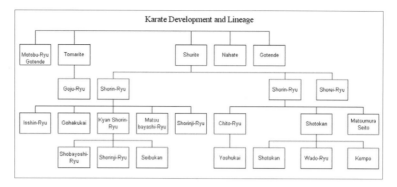

Shuri, Naha and Tomari were villages, from which the style names were derived.

We have not included the entirety of the styles within this matrix – rather, we have attempted to give you an insight into the development of some of the known styles you may have heard of.

All of the top-line styles (the originals) are collectively known as Koryu – meaning 'Old School'.

It may be interesting to you to note that the current Shotokan AND Wado-Ryu styles were developed from the original Shotokan and that Gichin Funakoshi Sensei had a direct influence on both!

It was during the 17th century that a law was introduced which prevented any Okinawan using or even owning a weapon.

The contravention of this law would result in severe punishment.

The local farmers and fishermen, fearing for their families, developed, predominantly in secret, their 'empty hand' fighting skills and the use of the tools of their respective trades (Nunchaku, Kama, Manriki Gusari, etc) for combat.

The Japanese Shogunate imposed further laws to completely eliminate the practice and deployment of the original Okinawan fighting systems.

The effect of this upon the development of Karate at this time had a profound consequence.

The practice and teaching of the art(s) was carried out in secret with only certain chosen individuals having the privilege of being able to learn this most secret fighting system.

The respective Kata, and particularly their application (Bunkai), were shrouded in utmost secrecy.

Effects of this have been carried forward into the Karate we practice today – many Sensei still do not know the original application of the techniques within a Kata.

One thing is certain: the techniques were of a most violent and brutal nature as their only purpose was to quickly, effectively and permanently defeat an opponent in combat.

From that which we have seen (and some deeper study of the styles), it is apparent that Karate as we know it today is a fusion of many different local forms from this era of Okinawan history.

The Masters of the time would gather, again in secret, to share the most effective application of their respective forms – a practice which is sadly lacking in today's society as secrecy and jealousy prevail unnecessarily.

Hachiman Symbol

The above symbol is the Ryukyu King's crest.

It is the War God symbol used by the Okinawan ruling family and also for our style:

Okinawan Koryu Karate-Jutsu – Okinawan Old School Empty Hand Science.

4.0 – Bunkai Jutsu

Parts of this section have used 'Unante', by John Sells, as research material - the Authors have interpreted and paraphrased this excellent historical study document for use in this publication.

We have previously mentioned the Oyo, the Henka and The Kakushi Waza.

A little more information on these, we feel, may prove beneficial to the serious Karateka although this section will be relatively short as we do not wish to overemphasize the metaphysical aspects of Karate.

All Karate and Kata practice intends, we believe, to expand, within the Karateka, the level of power, balance, focus, co-ordination and skill(s) of technique.

Kata are exercise and meditation in equal measure.

It should be noted, at this point, that today's means of Kata instruction and practice are much more relaxed than they once were.

The term 'Hito Kata San Nen' (One Kata Three Years) captures the requirement of the student mastering one kata before progressing to the next (although three years is probably an exaggeration of the reality, it is clear that much time was devoted to the perfection of the techniques of a single kata).

The Inner and the Outer Doctrines

The Inner doctrine
That appertaining to the hypothesis, application and understanding of Kata techniques:

Bunkai
This is the explanation of the techniques within a kata most often given and used for Kihon Ippons, Ippon Kumite and Kumite proper.

In Okinawa, this was known as Kumiti (the predecessor of Kumite and now unrelated to Kata practice – sadly).

Kakushite
This means 'Hidden Hand' and represents the covert purpose, concealed within the execution of the kata and not at once obvious in the physical effecting of the technique.

Jutsu
The Science of the application (to provide devastating effect).

Kakushite (or Kakushi Waza) should be encompassed by the Bunkai but, in today's Karate, it usually is not.

These are the deepest secrets (Gokui) hidden inside the posture and technique of the kata and conveyed from master to student.

The full realisation of this hypothesis is known as Oyo or Bunkai Oyo and, quite literally, means 'Practical Application' and covers the application of the technique(s) of the Kata as practised.

Henka or Bunkai Henka is the variation and change developed from the technique - just because in Kihon the fist is fully closed, this does not mean that, in application, Ippon Ken cannot be utilised.

Oyo and Henka, once Kakushi Waza have been fully considered, will provide the intermediate and conclusive techniques to defeat an opponent.

The Null Hypothesis of Bunkai is to understand the opposite of the technique within the Kata, that is to say, the technique against which the Karateka is defending.

Knowledge of this Ura Waza is the singular, most logical, aspect of the training.

The development of combative skills is inherent in the concept and Null Hypothesis of Ura Waza.

Also, within many Kata, is the representation of opposites - expressed by the repetition of techniques (block or strike).

Using this method of reverse technique, the Bunkai will be found hidden at the mid-point of the form – the point at which your opponent becomes transparent.

The Outer doctrine

That appertaining to the universal application of the principles of physical dynamics.

Kata Sequence and Pattern

Every Kata has a pre-set number of physical movements, carried out in a prescribed order.

No variations to this are allowed (subject to style variations).

The challenge here is not to improvise but to continually train for perfection.

Also the pattern or 'Embusen' is always, in part or totality, subject to an eight-directional line of movement and, with few exceptions, will end on the same spot as it began.

The Three Essential Points (Kata No San Yoso)

Mastery of this is prerequisite.

Wada No Dan Kyu	correct speed
Chikara No Kiyo-zaku	appropriate application of power
Karada No Shin-shiku	the graceful use of muscular tension

The above, obviously, relates to the performance of Kata and we're not going there on this occasion.

To finalise, the unification of both the Inner and Outer doctrines is an intensely idealistic, though comparatively indistinct, axiom, known, in Japanese, as Shuhari.

Shu means precise consideration of detail and prescribed custom (executing the Kata precisely as it was taught).

Ha means mastery of that custom.

Ri means to transcend the physical and be free from unnecessary movement and a graceful, or apparently unstructured, execution, unaffected by reticence.

It is to reach that which, articulated in old Okinawan, is:

Shimeijurasan

(A form of precision and exactitude that is the objective (although beyond reach) of all Martial Scientists.

Shuhari then, is a process through which an individual evolves.

It is not an 'immediate' torrent of wisdom.

The same is true when discussing, studying and understanding Kata, Bunkai Oyo, Bunkai Henka and Kakushite (Kakushi Waza).

5.0 – Kihon Kata

Kihon, quite literally, means 'basics or fundamentals' and has, for many years to our knowledge, been considered only this....basic!

We have photographically represented here each technique of Kihon Kata in its entirety.

Yoi Dachi

Look to left

Step and block (strike) Gedan Barai

Step through Oi Zuki Chudan

Look behind

Mawate Gedan Barai

Step through Oi Zuki Chudan

Look to left

Down middle Gedan Barai

Step Oi Zuki Chudan

Step Oi Zuki Chudan

Step Oi Zuki Chudan

Look to right

Mawate Gedan Barai

Step through Oi Zuki Chudan

Look behind

Mawate Gedan Barai

Step through Oi Zuki Chudan

Look left

Down middle Gedan Barai

Step Oi Zuki Chudan

Step Oi Zuki Chudan

Step Oi Zuki Chudan

Look right

Mawate Gedan Barai

Step through Oi Zuki Chudan

Look behind

Mawate Gedan Barai

Step through Oi Zuki Chudan

Yoi Dachi

a. Kihon – Oyo

The theory of ON and OFF-LINE response
is clearly displayed here.

Within the Kata itself, would you really stay on-line and expend energy
to 'block' an attack?

We believe that, as you are stepping either angular to or into an attack
(OFF-LINE), can this be considered defensive?

As shown, an angular step is used which enters the attacker's zone
(irimi) and strikes the Atemi on the arm.

Followed by a stepping punch to the head (Oi-Zuki Jodan).

The next two techniques merely repeat the above, with a possible 180
degree turn initially.

The Gedan Barai and three Oi-Zuki's, in our opinion, represent the 'follow-on' attack – once the attacker is retreating (most likely in pain), follow it up and finish the job.

The remainder of the techniques in Kihon, at the Oyo level, are self-explanatory.

Flawless execution, on both sides of the body, is paramount.

Many martial artists practice only on the 'strong' side of their body.

We believe that Kihon, at Oyo level, provides the foundation for multiple side efficiency of technique.

b. Kihon – Henka

Again, this technique begins with an angular entering of the attacker's zone, Gedan Uchi, quickly followed by an Atemi Uchi – Shuto Uchi – to the upper bicep of the attacking arm.

The attacking arm is then captured, rotated through 180 degrees, and used to manipulate the attacker to a point of total imbalance using force applied to the tricep muscle and local Atemi, whilst stepping back to a position of Gedan Barai.

A step through, incorporating a Hiza Geri to the Jodan region, is then executed, ending with a shoulder dislocation (Kaiten Nage).

Following on (down the middle), the movement of the Gedan Barai is actually a deflection with a rolling joint lock to the chest and, at the same time, a Tate Zuki to the Jodan region.

This is then swiftly followed by a rolling Tate Zuki (Hidari then Migi) with only one step to completion (Hidari Gyaku Tate Zuki to Migi Oi Tate Zuki).

In this next Kata sequence, the attack comes in the form of a shoulder grab in an attempt to turn the 'defender' on to a punch.

Obviously, the expectation is that the 'defender' will turn INTO the attack.

However, the 'defender' drops slightly and turns AWAY from the pull (opposite direction), strikes Tetsui Uchi to the floating ribs, and rises to either a) lock the arm (fingers could be trapped in clothing), or b) release the grab.

This is quickly followed by a stepping punch to the head (Oi Zuki Jodan).

Within Kihon, as stated previously, there is a certain amount of repetition.

The techniques are the same, up or down.

Obviously, we could add many more variations to these techniques. However, as space is restricted, we will leave well enough alone!

Your interpretation of the application of this Kata is just as valid as ours!

c. Kihon – Kakushi Waza

An attack with a knife (which we consider life-threatening and therefore will meet with extreme prejudice) begins this technique.

The attacker thrusts the knife to the chudan region.

The defender responds with an interceptory Gedan Barai to the attacking arm followed by a stepping strike (Teisho Uchi) to the head, at the same time grabbing the opponent's head (Teisho Uchi with the other hand to the chin).

This is quickly followed by Mawate into Gedan Barai, attacking the neck of the attacker, and a step through with a clearing technique (moving the attacker out of your zone in anticipation of another attack), with another Teisho Uchi or similar.

The mid-section of Bunkai-Jutsu for Kihon Kata again assumes that a knife is used in the attack due to the sticking hands (chin-na) element of the sequence but would be equally effective against any other attack, armed or not.

The initial attack is intercepted by a Gedan Uchi to the attacking arm, followed by a Gedan Shuto Uchi to the same arm.

The arm is then captured and turned into Ikkio, held Hidari-te, and the attacker is struck Migi Tate Zuki to the Jodan region.

The Tate Zuki attack is rolled back to the trapped arm as Osai Uchi with Hidari Teisho Uchi to the Jodan region.

The head is then grabbed (Hidari) as a base followed by a strike to the carotid artery with Migi Ippon ken.

The closing sequence is a little complicated but very effective.

The attack could be with a bat, shank, knife etc, and as such, an advantage is needed.

This advantage comes in the form of a low ura Mawashi Geri as a misdirectional attack to the knee region (anywhere from knee to mid-thigh will suffice).

This is followed by Hidari Tetsui Uchi to the head (if possible) which will further disorientate the attacker.

The climax of this technique is the grab of the head (right over left), turning (thus attacking the neck) and clearing.

Once the head is grabbed, pull down into Koshi Gamae Migi and continue the turn into Migi chudan Zuki.

Not pretty but it gets the job done!

As previously stated, the return sequence of the Kata is the same, on the opposite side for balance.

Kihon – Closing Comment

In our experience, Kihon is primarily taught as a 'basic' Kata, and once more advanced Kata has been learned, Karateka tend to view Kihon as too basic.

We hope and believe that we have shown here that even the humble Kihon is a complex, balanced and devastating Kata, and perhaps a well kept secret in the martial arts world.

We must all strive to understand the reason that this, and possibly all other Kata, was created in the first place.

If you take the time to study the techniques shown here for Kihon, you will see the diversity, complexity and wealth of knowledge which has been unleashed.

In addition, it is clear that these techniques would be equally effective against a fully armoured samurai as against the local 'head the ball' who wants some drug money on Saturday night and picks the wrong 'victim'.

Whatever your level in martial arts and however you choose to study, open your mind to the past and you will be rewarded beyond measure.

Keep reading!

6.0 – Uchinadi Pinan Shodan

Yoi Dachi
Perpetuity A

Look left
Perpetuity A

Pull down Koshi Gamae
Perpetuity A

Age Uke, Ude Uke, Nekoashidachi
Perpetuity A

Gyaku Zuki, Pull back left hand
Perpetuity A

Oi Tetsui Zuki
Perpetuity A

Koshi Gamae
Perpetuity A (Opp)

Age Uke, Ude Uke, Nekoashidachi
Perpetuity A (Opp)

Gyaku Zuki, Pull back right hand
Perpetuity A (Opp)

Oi Tetsui Zuki
Perpetuity A (Opp)

Turn to rear, Ude Uke
Perpetuity B

Mae Geri Chudan
Perpetuity B

Mawate Shuto Uke
Perpetuity B

Step Shuto Uke
Perpetuity C

Step again Shuto Uke
Perpetuity C

Step Oi Nukite
Perpetuity C

Look right
Perpetuity C

Mawate Shuto Uke
Perpetuity C

Step Shuto Uke, 45 degrees

Mawate Shuto Uke

Step Shuto Uke, 45 degrees

Ude Uke, Kosa Dachi
Perpetuity D

Ude Uke, Kosa Dachi (Front view)
Perpetuity D

Migi Ashi Mae Geri
Perpetuity D

Gyaku Zuki
Perpetuity D

Ude Uke, Kosa Dachi

Hidari Mae Geri

Gyaku Zuki

Migi Morote Zuki
Perpetuity E

Mawate Gedan Barai
Perpetuity E

Step Age Uke, 45 degrees
Perpetuity E

Mawate Gedan Bara

Step Age Uke, 45 degrees

Yoi Dachi

a. Uchinadi Pinan Shodan – Oyo

Perpetuity A

Acceptance of an attack is a major aspect of Bunkai – we believe that there is no purely defensive technique – in this example, the attack is accepted for two reasons: to break the attacker's posture and to position the arm for a counter strike (Atemi Waza). We will cover some aspects of Kyusho Jutsu (the attack of anatomically vulnerable points) throughout the book.

This attack will, in all likelihood, be followed by a further attack – a spontaneous reflex action, if you will – defended in this example with Age Uke.

The purpose is to further disrupt the posture of the attacker and to expose the arm to a particularly unpleasant joint attack (the arm is at its most vulnerable at this extremity of position) – following with an Atemi strike to the mid-section and a Tetsui Zuki to the temple (another anatomically vulnerable point).
It is known to us as a 'finisher'.

b. Uchinadi Pinan Shodan – Henka

Perpetuity A

In this example, a crossed wrist grab is the initial offensive. Dropping into nekoashidachi and applying a joint lock to the elbow provides the posture break and, if applied with force, will also displace the joint.

A rapid reversal of posture to disorientate the attacker and a further application of a joint lock is used (a movement not dissimilar to Ude Uke) to take the attacker beyond his point of balance and posture. The arm is raised on its way to apply a Kyusho strike to the mid-section or neck area prior to the final application of an entire arm lock and manipulation technique (Shiho Nage).

The left arm here is used as a cautious cover whist the right arm extends in the manner and with the velocity of a strike to takedown and, when grounded, is snapped back to the hip with a Shuto Uchi to the unlocked area of the neck. The result is devastating.

Follow-up techniques are not always necessary and, as in this instance, the attacker is so incapacitated by the ferocity of the response that no further controlled aggression is applied.

c. Uchinadi Pinan Shodan – Kakushi Waza

Perpetuity A

In this example, the application of the 'hidden' technique of Kata is more evident. As the double wrist grab is applied, presumably to be succeeded by an attack using an alternative part of the attacker's body, a drop into Koshi Gamae is used for the posture break.

The chin is dropped to lock the points around the neck, but this also doubles as a head-butt.

The same movement as a previous example is used for the wrist lock (Ikkio), but this time distance is closed quickly to maintain maximum pressure on the joint and to prevent retaliatory or reciprocal attacks.

The right hand is used to further increase effectiveness and to provide leverage for the follow-up technique.

A rapid and forceful projection of the attacker's arm causes muscle tearing and joint displacement to a grave degree, and leaves the attacker grounded and totally incapacitated. However, as this example represents the true combative nature of Kata, a finishing axe kick to the throat of the attacker completes this defence, with lethal force.

Note:
We, the authors of this work, do not condone unnecessary or unprovoked violence.

During these and forthcoming examples of Bunkai Jutsu, we seek only to enlighten with the evidence that the true application of Kata was devastating.

Only the minimal amount of controlled aggression should be required to bring most confrontations to a quick and merciful close. However, when these techniques were developed, mercy was in short supply as the originators were fighting for their lives.

Should your life be endangered during a confrontation, it is our opinion that NO FORCE SHOULD BE CONSIDERED EXCESSIVE.

a. Uchinadi Pinan Shodan – Oyo

Perpetuity B

This example is neither acceptance nor rejection – the neutral and disdainful indifference to an attack can only come with confidence and this can only be gained through faith and experience – faith in your skill and experience in your chosen area of study.

Here we see a counter to an anatomically vulnerable point, effectively closing down the arm and preventing a counter swing. A short, close-range Mae Geri is applied to the base of the rib cage, quickly followed by a Ushiro Empi Uchi to the same point or just above.

b. Uchinadi Pinan Shodan – Henka

Perpetuity B

In all instances, the most effective means of releasing a grab to the wrist is to apply pressure against the thumb – the weakest aspect of the grip.

In this example, slightly decreasing the distance acts as the posture break and unlocks certain points and anatomical areas.

A short Hara Mae Geri drops the attacker's head and closes most avenues of follow-up attack, and allows the left hand to be comfortably placed as the base for a Teisho strike to the point of the chin.

This interim strike will sufficiently disorientate the attacker to prevent resistance when the finishing neck attack (Toruguchi) is applied.

c. Uchinadi Pinan Shodan – Kakushi Waza

Perpetuity B

In this example, as previously, indifference is shown to the attack.

Distance judged against the counter offensive.

Ude Uchi could be applied to the temple of the attacker as a penetrative attack which causes disorientation. A firm grip on the shoulder (clothing) is established followed by a short Gedan Mae Geri to disrupt the attacker's posture and to drop backwards.

Whereupon, a Shuto Uke neck attack is applied as the finisher.

a. Uchinadi Pinan Shodan – Oyo

Perpetuity C

 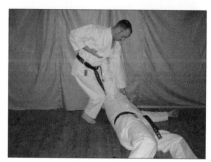

Intercepting attacks is another major aspect of Bushi-Jutsu.

In this case, the attack is intercepted using Migi Shuto Uchi to the bicep area, stepping through Hidari Shuto Uchi to the Jodan region, dropping the left arm to grab the right wrist and stepping through in the manner of Migi nukite and, grabbing the opponent's hair, clothing or around the neck, a turn through 270 degrees is then executed, followed by Koshi Nage, and two Shuto Uchi to the Jodan region.

b. Uchinadi Pinan Shodan – Henka

Perpetuity C

Physical manipulation of your opponent (and therefore knowledge of body physics) and where and how various parts of their bodies will react to techniques you apply is also extremely important.

In this instance, a swinging punch is the attack against which we 'cower' – we have found that this lulls the attacker into a false sense of security.

From this, we cover using the left hand and, with kake Uchi, strike the bicep area of the attacker's arm – we then capture the attacker's hand with our covering hand.

The hand is then twisted into Ikkio, which represents the second Shuto and is followed by a Teisho strike to the locked elbow joint (a variation of nukite, as represented in Kata).

c. Uchinadi Pinan Shodan – Kakushi Waza

Perpetuity C

This next sequence again assumes a knife attack (we can only assume!) and, as such, will feature a devastating retaliation, including some Kyusho Jutsu – we did warn you before you bought the book!

The attack swings inwards to slash and is met by a virtually simultaneous strike to the Atemi on the attacker's arm (lung four, heart five) and a Shuto Uchi to the Atemi on the neck (stomach 20).

The second Shuto (per the Kata), is actually a base grab to the hair on the top of the attacker's head, pulling the head backwards to reveal the front of the throat and to unlock the attacker's Atemi.

The nukite (per the Kata) is actually a crushing Shuto Uchi to this very vulnerable area – this technique is likely to cause a fatality.

As usual, the next sequence (Shuto Uchi and 45 degrees) is merely the repetition of technique in order on ensure balance is maintained.

a. Uchinadi Pinan Shodan – Oyo

Perpetuity D

This sequence is carried out, mostly, in Kosa Dachi.

The reason for this, we believe, is the fact that Kosa Dachi is a naturally balanced stance which your body will adopt instinctively when off balance or moving quickly.

When you are drunk (we're sure it's not very often!), you will 'stagger' into Kosa Dachi.

When the boxer 'back-pedals' in the ring, he will use Kosa Dachi.

If a hook or right-cross is thrown, the technique will end in Kosa Dachi. This stance is often overlooked but is actually a very balanced and solid stance for combat.

The attack is in the form of Mae Geri, Oi Zuki.

The defence is a step off-line into Hidari Kosa Dachi (to avoid the Mae Geri) and a Ude Uke to block the Oi Zuki.

A counter Mae Geri is applied followed by a drop into Gyaku Zuki.

The targets will be whatever is accessible during the confrontation.

b. Uchinadi Pinan Shodan – Henka

Perpetuity D

Henka sees the same attack with a varied response, in the form of a Ude Uchi to the tricep of the attacking arm (to deaden the limb), quickly followed by a shoulder grab – all still in Kosa Dachi.

The reason for the grab is to pull the attacker onto the counter attack.

Pulling the attacker onto the Mae Geri will have a more devastating effect than allowing them to 'ride' the blow – likewise, maintaining the grab for the Gyaku Tate Zuki will have a similarly devastating effect.

The target areas for the strikes, again, are any which are vulnerable at the time.

c. Uchinadi Pinan Shodan – Kakushi Waza

Perpetuity D

Using the same attack sequence again, Kakushi Waza uses Ude Uchi to the vulnerable points of the head or neck – again, in Kosa Dachi.

This is followed by a base grab (hair, collar, shoulder, neck etc) and a Hiza Geri to the floating ribs into a Mae Fumikomi to either leg (depending on your reach) directly to the knee joint (this follows the leg to the floor and shatters the knee cap).

This will unlock all of the vulnerable points on the attacker's back and allow a multitude of devastating counters – we have chosen a Gyaku Tate Zuki to the spinal column – we think that the effect here is quite obvious!

a. Uchinadi Pinan Shodan – Oyo

Perpetuity E

Same again for the other side.

The following sequence begins with Morote Uke from an attacking punch.

This may be a little controversial but, if we're all honest, we will see the truth in it.

We may all like to think that our techniques ALWAYS work but we all know that this is not the case.

There are times when our techniques don't work out quite the way we imagined.

In this case, the Morote Uke is actually a grab for a Koshi Nage (hip throw) but the throw has not been effective.

WHAT DO WE DO?

PANIC?

No….gedan Tetsui Uchi to the groin followed by a Age Uchi to the chin should have the effect we want.

b. Uchinadi Pinan Shodan – Henka

Perpetuity E

The Henka for this sequence is what we call a 'wailer'.

We believe that Morote Uke is not an assisted block.

WHAT IS THE POINT OF THAT?

We believe (and have shown) that the 'assisting' hand is actually the blocking hand, and the 'blocking' hand is actually the striking hand – therefore we block, strike, strike, strike – wailing!

Morote Uchi (not Uke) is the block and strike, followed by Gedan Tetsui Uchi and Age Uchi – simplicity.

c. Uchinadi Pinan Shodan – Kakushi Waza

Perpetuity E

A little more complicated – the first technique – morote Uchi – could be a defence against a punch or a knife attack – we have chosen a knife attack to demonstrate effect.

The 'blocking' hand, this time, becomes the grasping hand (or sticking hand); the striking hand is still the striking hand but also grabs the head after the strike.

The next technique uses aspects of irimi Nage and kote gaeshi to take the attacker to ground in a locked state.

The Age Uchi, in this Bunkai, actually shatters the arm whilst striking the attacker's Atemi around the head and neck area.

It may be necessary to change posture to accommodate the counter. However, we must all remember that Kata is the STYLISED version of the actual science of the technique – Kata looks good – Bunkai devastates.

Uchinadi Pinan Shodan – Closing Comment

As previously stated, we cannot excuse unnecessary violence.

The techniques in this book are primarily intended as a source of study for the serious martial artist.

We had become disillusioned with the constant disregard of Kata as a 'boring necessity' of a Karate class.

With so much emphasis today on sport Karate and Kumite, we felt that the time was right to introduce a book which will undoubtedly cause controversy and debate, but which will also enlighten and inspirit those who read it to undertake their own journey of discovery.

We feel that we have shown here that even the humble Pinan Shodan (in addition to the humble Kihon) can be a Kata of devastating effect if the time is taken to interpret the technique within it.

This version of Pinan Shodan (Uchinadi) is ancient, perhaps dating back to the origins of origin (but who can really tell?).

Some other versions we have seen have been further altered and the techniques have become lost in the mists of time.

Use your own insight into your art and your own interpretation of the techniques to arrive at the most effective technique possible for your body type.

The body physics we have applied to this and all other Kata within this book are those which suit each one of us individually.

NOTHING is cast in stone.

The purpose of this book is simple and modest.

Guidance.

7.0 – Uchinadi Pinan Nidan

Yoi Dachi
Perpetuity A

Look left
Perpetuity A

Pull down Koshi Gamae
Perpetuity A

Hidari Uraken, Nekoashidachi
Perpetuity A

Step through Migi Oi Zuki
Perpetuity A

Look behind
Perpetuity A

*Mawate, Migi Gedan Barai,
Moto Dachi
Perpetuity A*

*Pull Back Migi Uraken,
Nekoashidachi
Perpetuity A*

*Step through Hidari Oi Zuki
Perpetuity A*

Look left

*Turn to left, Hidari Gedan Barai
Perpetuity B*

*Step through Migi Age Uke
Perpetuity B*

Step through, Hidari Age Uke
Perpetuity B

Step through Migi Age Uke
(rise as technique ends)
Perpetuity C

Look right
Perpetuity C

Mawate Hidari Gedan Barai
Perpetuity C

Step through Migi Oi Zuki
Perpetuity C

Look behind
Perpetuity C

Mawate Migi Gedan Barai

Step through Hidari Oi Zuki

Look left

*Turn left, Hidari Gedan
Barai Moto Dachi
Perpetuity D*

*Step through Migi Oi Zuki
Perpetuity D*

*Step through Hidari Oi Zuki
Perpetuity D*

Step through Migi Oi Zuki
(rise as technique ends)
Perpetuity D

Look right (reverse view)

Mawate Hidari Gedan Shuto Uke

Step Migi Gedan Shuto Uke,
45 degrees

Look behind
Perpetuity E

Mawate Migi Gedan Shuto Uke
Perpetuity E

Step Migi Gedan Shuto Uke,
45 degrees

Yoi Dachi

a. Uchinadi Pinan Nidan – Oyo

Perpetuity A

The attack is in the form of a wrist grab (same or opposite side) to the left arm.

The immediate response is top step off-line, pull down in to Koshi Gamae, and strike towards the attacker's head (contact is a bonus!).

This breaks the attacker's posture and unlocks the anatomically vulnerable areas of the attacker's anatomy.

Step through and punch through the attacker's head (or choose your own target!).

b. Uchinadi Pinan Nidan – Henka

Perpetuity A

In this example, an opposite side wrist grab is used to the right arm or a same side wrist grab to the right arm.

Again, step off-line, pull down into Koshi Gamae, and place the attacker into a wrist lock.

(1. Same side = Ikkio, 2. Opposite side = Kote Gaeshi)

Step through and strike Oi Zuki – again, choose your own target area.

c. Uchinadi Pinan Nidan – Kakushi Waza

Perpetuity A

In this example, same side wrist grab to the left arm is the attack.

Strike Shuto across the attacker's wrist, grab it and pull back into Koshi Gamae (trapping the attacker's arm with your arm).

Strike Gedan Tetsui Uchi to the attacker's facial region, pull back Osai Uke to the attacker's elbow joint and shatter the arm.

Hiza Geri to the attacker's head, as you step in, maintain the lock, Mawate and take your attacker to ground (pull back and up as you complete the technique).

This will expose a variety of vulnerable points.

The finisher here is a sokuto Geri to any vulnerable point exposed.

In lay-man's terms – stamp kick to the attacker's rib cage would be very effective.

PLEASE BE AWARE, A STAMP KICK TO ANY REGION EXPOSED DURING THIS TECHNIQUE WILL HAVE DEVASTATING EFFECTS.

TO THE RIBS, PUNCTURED LUNGS.

TO THE THROAT, CRUSHED WIND-PIPE/ARTERIES.

TO THE FACE/HEAD, SERIOUS CRANIAL TRAUMA.

The remaining techniques of Pinan Nidan (gedan Barai, three Age Uke down the centre, Mawate Gedan Barai, Oi Zuki, Mawate Gedan Barai, Oi Zuki, Mawate Gedan Barai, three Oi Zuki down the centre) can be interpreted in the same way as Kihon Kata (substitute the Oi Zuki of Kihon with the Age Uke of Nidan for your own application) with the obvious exception of the closing moves.

For the closing moves of Nidan, the following application can apply:

a. Uchinadi Pinan Nidan – Oyo

Perpetuity E

The attack is in the form of an underarm knife stab.

The initial Gedan Shuto is Uke to the attacking arm, followed by a step-in and Gedan Shuto Uchi to the attacker's groin area.

b. Uchinadi Pinan Nidan – Henka

Perpetuity E

In this example, the attack is from a wrist grab to the leading (left) arm (probably closely followed by a punch or head-butt).

The equaliser and posture breaker is a simultaneous strike and rejection technique (mae Teisho Uchi with the right hand and Mawashi Empi Uke with the left hand to reject the grab).

This is closely followed by Gedan Shuto Uchi to the attacker's groin area and a slight angular step (45 degrees) to unlock the vulnerable points around the head and neck area, and provide an opportunity for the second and final Gedan Shuto Uchi.

c. Uchinadi Pinan Nidan – Kakushi Waza

Perpetuity E

In this final example, a same side wrist grab is the attack.

This attack is accepted (as opposed to rejected as in the Henka) and is balanced by the equalising hand – this represents the first Gedan Shuto Uke.

The second Gedan Shuto Uke is represented by the rotation under the arm and grab of the attacker's arm.

The full application of this technique is the sudden reversal of force in the grab – the effect is shattering.

8.0 – Effective Punching

Theory

As serious students of Bushi Jutsu, we have opted to study all of the facets which make, what we consider to be, a fully rounded warrior.

In so doing, we have had cause to question all of the current beliefs which exist in all of the combative arts.

We have studied the cross, hook, upper-cut and jab of boxing.

We have studied the Oi Zuki, Gyaku Zuki, Mawashi Zuki, Kizami Zuki and Kage Zuki of Karate.

We have studied the Chin-Na of Gong Fu.

We have studied the Lightning Hands of Bagua.

As a result of this extensive study, we have deduced a number of truths.

In a 'real' combat situation, the strikes of boxing are inappropriate, the strikes of Karate are too long and stylised, the Chin-Na will only work with opponent co-operation, and the lightning hands of bagua are 'Hollywood' fantasy.

The following section will concern itself with our interpretation of effective punching without the ego!

A common misconception, particularly in untrained punchers, is that you need to throw a punch from somewhere near your toes in order to generate the power required for the punch to be effective.

Alternatively, an effort is made to throw the punch from as far back around the body as possible.

In either case, it would probably be easier and safer to send your opponent a postcard telling him that the punch is on its way or wear a large neon sign around your neck which says: I AM GOING TO THROW A PUNCH NOW!

How this type of brawler ever manages to land a punch is a complete mystery to us!

Furthermore, the orientation of the fist and the contact area have a massive influence on the effectiveness of the punch.

Power Generation

During the initial stages of instruction of a new student, we always try to communicate the need to use body weight as the best method of adding effect to a thrown punch.

Whether this is in the application of a step behind a punch or the thrust of a hip, the principle is comparable and sound.

At a higher level, the hip thrust and body weight transfer are only a small part of the overall generation of punching power.

Monkey puncher

Round the block puncher

The images above demonstrate the typical 'monkey puncher' and 'round the block' puncher.

Clearly, this type of excessive motion power generation is far too indicative of intended action – remember the postcard and the neon sign?

Also, have you noticed the orientation of the fist in both cases?

Mid-punch position

Contact position (1)

Contact position (2)

Two points; which portion of the fist will make contact and who will be the one most seriously hurt?

Consider the following posture and distancing as an alternative to the above.

Posture

Distance

Orientation

Contact

How is the power generated?

This is a principle we call 'Triangulation' – this will be explained in further detail during the section on locks and control later. However, for now, the triangles we are talking about are better shown than described – see below.

Triangle A

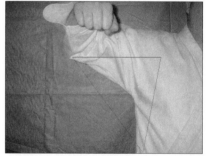

Triangle B

For a hook, for example, the smaller triangle 'A' is, the more power can be generated. However, triangle 'B' must be quite extended.

For a straight punch, however, 'A' starts small and extends whilst 'B' stays small throughout.

Both of these scenarios are depicted below.

Common   *Studied*

Hook 1   *Hook 2*

Straight 1   *Straight 2*

Enough of the generalisations.

    Let's look at the comparisons of the following strikes:

    Hook (Kage Zuki, Mawashi Zuki)

    Cross (Mawashi Zuki)

    Straight (Oi Zuki, Gyaku Zuki)

    Jab (Kizami Zuki)

    Back Fist (Uraken).

    Upper Cut (Ura Zuki).

Common   *Studied*

A. Hook

B. Cross

C. Straight

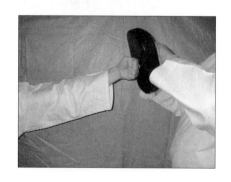

D. Jab

Common   *Studied*

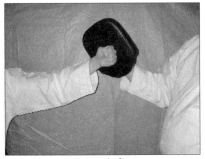

E. Back fist

F. Upper cut

Let's also look at the postures they are thrown from:

A. Hook

Common   *Studied*

B. Cross

C. Straight

D. Jab

Common	Studied

E. Back fist

F. Upper cut

Combat Punching

We practice and study classical Karate.

We have found, during the course of this study, that the classical Karate 'corkscrew' punch is not effective in a real combat situation.

There are a number of reasons for us making this statement.

Firstly, the most direct route between two points is a straight line – this is basic physics and geometry.

Why then would we expend energy 'twisting' a punch in mid throw?

If we look at an analogy, imagine hammering a nail into a piece of wood.

Would you twist the hammer away prior to striking the nail….and still expect to generate the same forces to drive the nail into the wood?

Obviously, you would begin the hammer blow with the hammer orientated in the correct manner in order to generate as much power as possible.

Exactly the same principle applies to punching.

Secondly, the distance from which the punch must travel is far too great to be effective.

We tend to 'cower' when approached by a potential aggressor (see image).

Cower (front)

Cower (side)

From the 'cower', the combat punch (short-range Tate-Zuki) can be thrown with incredible power and speed.

The following images show the contact of a combat punch against pads.

Focus pad 1

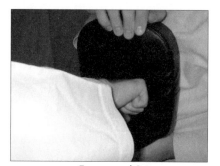
Focus pad 2

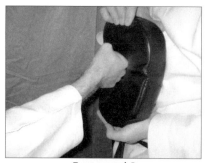
Focus pad 3

Furthermore, if we look at the lineage of the classical punch (see image), it is very obvious where the weak intersection points are.

The wrist, elbow and shoulder intersections are forced into an unnatural state.

Classical lineage   *Combat lineage*

If you then compare this to the combat posture, you will see that the wrist is now directly in line, the elbow has rotated to a position of strength, and the shoulder has dropped back into its natural state.

The net effect of this is that, in a more natural and relaxed state, the punch will travel faster, with more power and with far less risk of injury.

Isn't that what we train for?

Punching (additional)

The three stages of the reverse punch:

- The first stage (close range) can be expressed as Sakasa Zuki (inverted punch).
  This is delivered direct to the target, without any twist being applied – this way, at this range, maximum power can be generated.
- At medium (mid) range, the punch will become Tate Zuki (vertical punch).
  In real combat, 95% of situations will become physical at this range – we believe that this punch is one of the most powerful and penetrative of the human arsenal.
- At long range (arm's distance), the punch becomes Gyaku Zuki (reverse punch).
  We, as previously stated, believe that, even at this range, Tate Zuki is probably equalling, if not exceeding, the power of a fully rotated Gyaku Zuki and is our preferred striking media.

All of this is dependent upon Ma-ai (proper distance).

Additionally, within a movement such as Gyaku Zuki (full motion), you will also find grappling techniques, wrist/joint locks, throws and others.

So, in actual fact, it should be called Gyaku Waza (reverse techniques) because what we actually practice is only a punch if viewed with blinkered vision.

Also, remember that the striking techniques found within Kata are exclusively intended for bare fist striking flesh application.

The principle of competition punching, in a ring, wearing gloves, is entirely different to that which we are studying here.

9.0 – Effective Kicking

Theory

As with the punching aspects of our study, we have similarly discounted a large proportion of the classical kicking techniques of Karate and other striking arts.

In a 'live' street situation, any kick above waist height is simply not effective.

Why?

The answer is simple – posture.

Now, most 'kickers' will vehemently disagree with this, saying that their kicks are powerful enough or fast enough or 'whatever'; this is, of course, absolute rubbish.

In a Gi, there is enough material around the groin to allow unrestricted high kicks. However, what about in your favourite Levi's 501's and your Rockports?

We actually do head kicks but this invariably follows a kick to the calf or knee or thigh muscle or groin etc; bringing the head to the foot, rather than the foot to the head.

We suggest a short experiment.

Find a partner roughly your height and weight and stand face to face.

Ask your partner to perform a fast but controlled head kick – front leg or back.

You will out-pace the head kick with a punch, everytime.

Try it!

If you can't, maybe you should consider cookery instead!

The point here is not to suggest punching instead of kicking – kicking does have a place in modern combat – the point is to encourage the use of effective kicks instead of the film star rubbish.

Power Generation

The power of a kick tends to be generated through the hips.

Whether front, back, side or round doesn't matter.

Power, however, is lost if a kick has to be extended higher than the waist, as a fair proportion of the energy is used up in achieving the height and looking fancy.

We tend to use three basic kicks in combat situations, as follows:

Kick 1 – low level Mawashi Geri

| Front view | Side view |

This kick can be used to attack either the front leg or the back leg.

If applied with enough force, the back leg attack can result in the attacker hitting the ground very forcibly.

This kick (along with the other two) can be thrown very quickly from a 'cowered' posture.

Kick 2 – low level, close range Mae Geri

| Front view | Side view |

This kick can be used in very tight, close quarter combat situations.

It can be thrown from virtually nose-to-nose and any distance away up to a 'cowered' posture.

The effect of this kick, well placed on the knee-cap, is hurtful.

Kick 3 – low level Kosa Geri

Front view

Side view

This kick utilises the heel as the main contact point of the strike and, as with the above kick, well placed on the shin-bone or knee-cap, this kick is extremely effective.

You may have noticed that, when all three types are looked at, they utilise most of the striking points of the foot (1 uses the instep, two uses the ball of the foot (or toes, if you're wearing shoes), and three uses the heel and inside arch of the foot).

We do also use low-level, short-range side kicks and stamping kicks, but these tend to be more useful as finishers (a stamping kick to a vulnerable area whilst grounded is devastating).

In closing, a combination of close-range, low-level kicks followed by short-range direct punches can end a conflict within seconds.

The essence of combat – speed, power and effect.

10.0 – Effective Striking

In this section, we will cover the following strikes and types of strikes:

- Knee strikes
- Head strikes
- Elbow strikes
- Arm strikes
- Hand strikes:
    - Fingers
    - Palms
    - Slaps (front and back)
    - Wrist strikes

Knee Strikes

The classical Hiza Geri is woefully underused as a combative weapon.

Its use is slightly selective but, if it can be used, particularly to the head or neck, its effect is closure.

It has also been misinterpreted as only a strike when it can be used as a pressure or impact attack (see example).

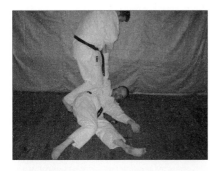

Obviously, this is not an exhaustive list – it is just a few examples of how the knee can be used in combat.

Head Strikes

Before we outline the use of the head as a striking weapon, it should be pointed out that there is a level of risk involved.

If the strike is mistimed or misjudged, it can cause injury to both yourself and your opponent.

It must therefore be used selectively or when no other course of action is available.

The contact point of the head is critical (see example).

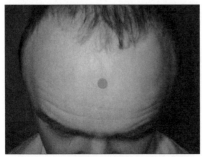
Front view

Side view

Also, the manner in which the head is used is also critical.

Most people tend to lift the chin when preparing to throw the head or turn the chin sideways away from their opponent.

In both cases, your eyes leave your opponent and you show your intent – this is the cardinal sin.

You must never show your opponent what your attack is likely to be and you should never allow your focus to be interrupted.

The correct way to strike with the head is shown below.

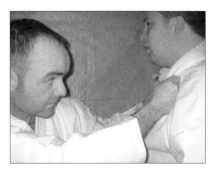

We must, again, stress that this is a selective or 'no option' technique rather than a first choice.

Elbow Strikes

The elbow is probably one of the most devastating weapons in the human armoury.

It can be used from mid to close range, on hard or soft targets, for reaction or total devastation and, in the right circumstances with the appropriate level of body physics knowledge, it can be fatal.

We have tried to show (over leaf) a variety of elbow strikes to a variety of targets.

Obviously, we cannot show ALL of the variations as we would need a separate book for this.

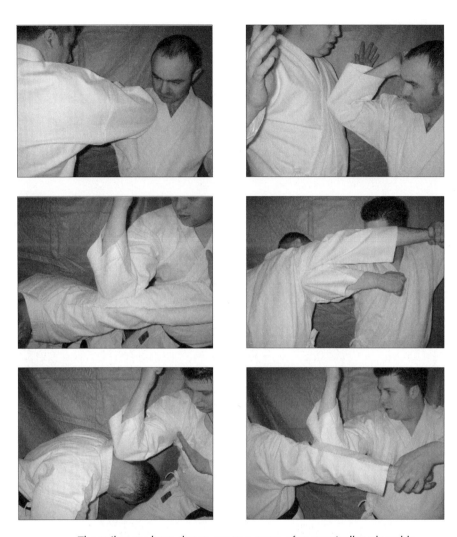

The strikes we have shown are to a range of anatomically vulnerable targets but they can be to any target – the versatility of this strike is incomparable.

There are other, hidden, uses of this technique (Kakushi Waza) which you will see in the following sections.

Arm Strikes

Arm strikes are another misunderstood concept of combat.

It doesn't HAVE to be a clenched fist or hard elbow or tensed foot for it to be an effective strike.

For example:

- Age Uke
- Soto Uke

- Ude Uke
- Shuto Uke
- Haito
- Irimi Nage
- Tenchi Nage

So, the first four are blocks, aren't they?

　　Maybe not – this section is about strikes so, should we take them out?

　　....or should we call them Uchi, not Uke?

　　....and what about haito – this is te Uchi isn't it?

　　Would you really strike someone with the inside edge of your hand?

　　The last two are Aikido throws aren't they?

　　Same question – should they be called Uchi and not Nage?

　　Here are some photos – you decide:

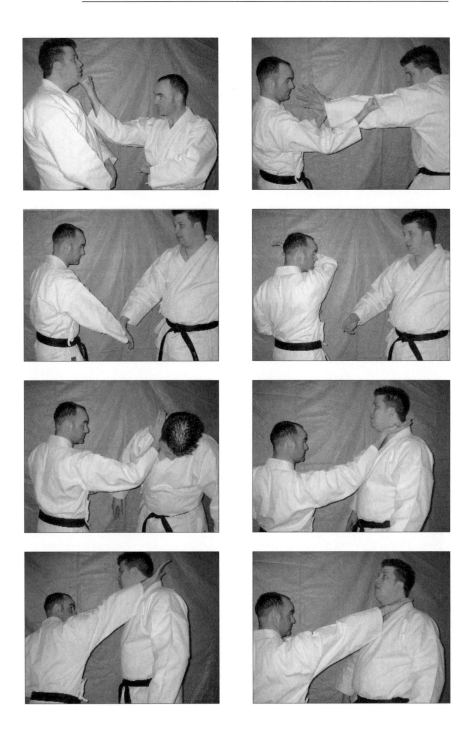

Hand Strikes

Fingers

Is it really effective to use the fingers to strike your opponent?

We have all heard stories about how the old masters conditioned their fingers by plunging them into hot sand, pebbles, shells etc, and maybe they did, but do we?

Can you honestly state that you can cause injury by striking an opponent with nukite or Ippon nukite or nihon nukite other than by striking vulnerable areas?

We believe that you can't, consistently.

You may get a lucky break occasionally but you will not sustain this type of strike due to the culture gap between modern fighters and ancient warriors and the risk of injury.

To us, it's fun – to them it was life or death.

So, we won't be showing how to pierce quarter inch plate steel with your fingers.

We won't even be showing you mystical finger movements which generate power and enlightenment.

In fact, we won't be showing you anything to do with finger striking as we cannot accept that it is a viable form of effective striking for combat.

There will be those who argue that finger and thumb strikes have their place.

We would not argue with this – their place is in a movie.

In the real world, you will probably cause yourself far more injury than your opponent.

The use, for example, of Ippon ken is said to be for precision attack.

In the heat of a real confrontation, on the streets, there is no time for precision other than to hit the general target you intended (head, ribs, groin etc).

If you think that you can reliably hit a target a half inch in diameter whilst your opponent is dumping adrenaline into his system and trying to rip your head off, then you live in cloud cuckoo land.

....and why would you want to try?

Pick any target you would choose to hit with Ippon ken and you will fare far better with a closed fist, short or long range.

For training in classical styles, Ippon ken and the rest are fine for refinement of technique, understanding of the principles of striking with such techniques, and practising in the Dojo. However, this book is about combat science so, if you want lies and exaggeration, probably best to put this book down and find something on one of the other mainstream styles.

There is a section, coming up, which focuses on the use of fingers and thumbs in combat.

It's not striking but that doesn't make it any less effective.

Palms

We feel that, as previously stated, anything you can strike with a palm you can just as effectively strike with a closed fist.

There are, however, exceptions to this general rule.

These exceptions are:

1. Hard – soft – soft – hard
2. Palm strike to grab
3. Front palm and reverse palm slaps

1. Hard – soft – soft – hard

The general principle of this is that when striking a hard target, use a soft technique (such as Teisho Uchi), and when striking a soft target, use a hard technique (such a Tate Zuki).

The following images show the variations.

Top of head

Forehead

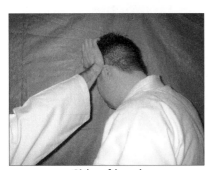

Side of head

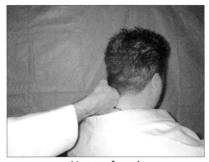

Nape of neck

Chin

Palm strike to grab

This can be used to make a point more so than to seriously injure or incapacitate your opponent.

The technique is applied when the contact is made with the front of the throat – the contact of the throat with the hand acts as a switch, causing the grab to be applied – see the following images:

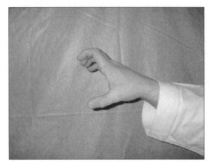

Hand orientation

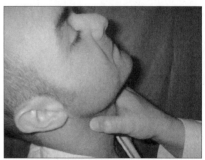

Contact point with throat

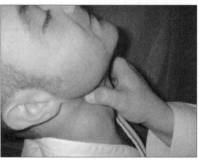

Grab

Front and reverse palm slaps

These slapping techniques, if performed correctly, are as effective as some punches.

The front palm slap is effectively a Teisho strike – this provides the effect of an otherwise girly technique.

The reverse palm slap, however, is by far the more effective of the two – see the images below:

Starting position

First stage of motion

Mid stage of motion

Contact point

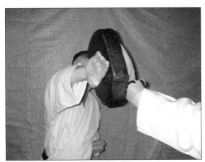

Contact point close-up

Ending position

This technique MUST be performed in a relaxed state.

As with all strikes, the end point is FAR past the intended target and the effect of the technique is derived from the fluid motion of the hand, arm and body, working together.

We recommend you try this technique using focus pads – you will be amazed at its effectiveness.

11.0 – When a Block is not a Block

At a combat level, we believe that a block is NEVER a block. That is not to say that all so-called blocks are strikes.

Some so-called blocks are posture breaks.

Others are muscle and joint manipulation techniques.

Others still are throws and yet others are weapon orientated techniques.

We'll try to explain:

In ALL of our Kata, from the 'lowest' to the 'highest', no opening technique is performed 'on-line' or stepping away from an assumed attack.

ALL of the opening techniques either step off-line or towards an opponent.

This logically assumes that, if you are stepping forward, you are attacking, not blocking, and if you are stepping off-line, you are moving away from an assumed attack so there is no need to block it, it's not going to hit you anymore.

So, when we teach Kihon Ippon to our students, they are taught to either step angular from a linear attack or, if remaining linear, intercept.

This can include Ude Uchi, soto Uchi, Age Uchi, Shuto Uchi or any other so-called block you can think of, incorporated as anything but a block.

The following images will demonstrate (with some sequences/combos):

Ude Uchi variation 1

Ude Uchi variation 2

Ude Uchi variation 3

Soto Uchi variation 1a

Soto Uchi variation 1b

Soto Uchi variation 1c

Soto Uchi variation 2a

Soto Uchi variation 2b

Soto Uchi variation 2c

Soto Uchi variation 2d

Age Uchi variation 1

Age Uchi variation 2

Age Uchi variation 3

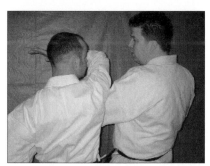

Shuto Uchi variation 1

Shuto Uchi variation 2

Shuto Uchi variation 3

Obviously, these examples are but a few of the potential range of application of so-called blocks.

The only restriction is the mind of the individual.

If your mind is closed, your growth in the martial sciences will be restricted.

If your mind is open, the boundaries are limitless.

12.0 – Throws, Locks, Control, Takedowns and Groundwork Principles

An Introduction

Throws

We do not believe that, in real combat, throws work cleanly. In most real street situations, the confrontation begins standing and very quickly goes to ground **most of the time!**

This is not the exception, it is the rule.

The myth of one-punch knockouts are exactly that – they rarely happen.

The so-called street fighter would like you to believe that it is a common occurrence but the reality is a little different.

The key to this is to be in control of the 'throw' so that you have the advantage once you reach the floor.

A throw then, to us, is more of a controlled but dynamic posture break.

The traditional throws of Judo have little street effect as some of them endanger the defender more than the attacker.

The stylised and dramatic throws of Aikido are similarly dependent on the attacker being co-operative – this will NEVER happen in a real combat situation.

We have seen demonstrations of Aikidoka who apparently throw their opponent using their index fingers only.

This is total rubbish.

If the attacker is willing to be thrown this way, it will look like it worked.

Out on the streets, you would have those fingers ripped off!

The common factor of these two martial arts is that they are both Do – the most simplistic form and that which has been watered down from the original, Jutsu – the Science.

Locks, Control and Takedown

We have so many effective variations that we would need a whole book dedicated just to this. However, we do not lock.

We pass through the locking stage of some techniques as we move into the shatter stage.

We make no apologies for what we are about to show.

The techniques we have found within the Kata were intended ONLY to PERMANENTLY disable the attacker.

NOT LOCK.

Our techniques destroy joints, muscles and soft tissues.

To uphold law and order, the techniques can be modified to be less brutal but they are NOT INTENDED TO BE USED AS LOCKS!

Following are some examples of this.

GREAT CARE SHOULD BE TAKEN WHEN PRACTISING THESE TECHNIQUES.

Example 1a

Example 1b

Example 1c

Example 1d

Example 1e

Example 2a

Example 2b

Example 2c

Example 2d

Example 2e

Example 3a

Example 3b

Example 3c

Example 3d

Example 3e

Example 3f

Example 4a

Example 4b

Example 4c

Example 4e

Example 4e

Example 5a

Example 5b

Example 5c

Example 5d

Example 6a

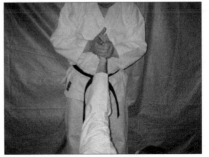

Example 6b

Example 6c

Example 6d

Example 6e

Example 6f

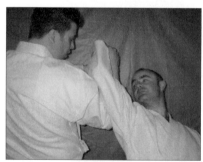

Example 6g

Example 6h

The control aspect of these techniques is self-explanatory.

When you are on the receiving end of these techniques, you will agree to just about anything if the pain will stop.

When these techniques are applied, the attacker can be moved forward or back, up or down, with the slightest application of the technique.

Most importantly, the attacker can be taken to ground whilst you maintain your control (and feet, if you wish).

Finally, when the technique is fully applied, the attacker will become a writhing mass of pain at your feet.

Job done.

Groundwork

In most confrontations we have witnessed, if both fighters end up on the ground, unless one of them takes immediate control, there will be a mad scramble to get back up.

This is normal human behaviour.

The best way to be the victor in this type of confrontation is the be the fighter in control on the ground.

If you can perform a takedown, you are automatically in control.

If, however, you are grappled to the ground, you may not be and will need to take control very quickly.

There are some basic principles which will help you to achieve this.

They are:

Never be underneath.

If you find yourself in this unfortunate position, the following techniques could be applied:

Dangerous starting position
(attacker above)

Pull down 1

Pull down 2

Full assault

Transfer 1

Transfer 2

Transfer 3

Transfer 4

Anything goes

Keep your centre of gravity as low as possible (this will stop you getting transferred (see above)).

Spread 1

Spread 2

Use everything at your disposal

If a handy house-brick is nearby, it can make a formidable weapon.

The time for honour and integrity has passed when you are fighting for your life, and if your attacker has his friends with him and you are on the floor, you will be.

Example 1 (Cell phone)

Example 2 (Car key)

Example 3 (Kneel on head)

Example 4 (Attack throat)

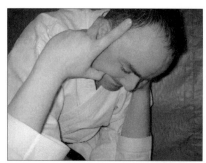 

Example 5 (Hook mouth)   *Example 6 (Use convenient ears)*

13.0 – Scripted Human Behaviour

I (DW) have studied psychology in an attempt to understand why people behave in the way in which they invariably do.

I have deduced many interesting facts from my studies – none more so than the fact that the invariability I mention above I now call 'Scripted Human Behaviour' – or SHB.

All humans, in given circumstances, will behave in a reliably predictable way – this is the script (for the situation).

Haven't you ever opined privately or even said:

'If that was me, I'd have done this?'

Chances are, you'd have behaved in exactly the same way the other person did – UNLESS YOU HAVE CONDITIONED YOURSELF TO RESPOND OUTSIDE THE SCRIPT.

This can be the difference between victory and defeat, and applies to ALL ASPECTS OF OUR LIVES.

Obviously, we will be concerning ourselves only with the involuntary responses which pertain to interpretation and application of Kata.

The creators of the original Kata were great observers of reactionary stimuli and, as such, were able to see psychosomatic responses of individuals in a combat scenario.

The Kata themselves, therefore, are extremely well equipped to utilise the involuntary responses to attacks to certain anatomically vulnerable points.

The need to study the Kata for this is very obvious.

Most Karateka will not even be aware of SHB, let alone be able to use it to their advantage in combat.

Can it be relied upon?

It is probably the single most reliable aspect of Kata (other than its effectiveness if correctly interpreted).

If you grip someone's wrist in an aggressive manner, they will tense up and try to pull away.

If you strike the groin, they will curl up and back away.

If you grab the lapels (or that general area) they will try to pull away.

If you pull the hair (thus the head) in a direction, the body will attempt to follow, even if it means sacrificing balance, posture and position.

If a punch is thrown, the opponent will cower.

These are untrained, involuntary responses – the opponent will no more be aware of them than he/she is aware of breathing, pulse and heartbeat.

When these responses can be predicted and seized as an advantage, then the outcome of the confrontation can probably be predicted as favourable.

As Kata is utilising these responses, if is fair to assume that its intended use is to incapacitate untrained aggressors but is this really so?

When the Samurai, escaping the wars, took Okinawan wives who then bore children, were these children taught only the ways of the Okinawan systems or the then new hybrid incorporating the ways of the Samurai (armed and un-armed).

We believe it is far more likely to be the latter (which is why you will be able to see the avoidance of strikes to armoured areas and why, in a forthcoming publication, we will be looking at convert and overt weaponry, as did the Samurai of old).

If you find yourself attacked by a trained fighter, your emphasis should shift from utilising involuntary responses to utilising known, trained responses.

A generic understanding of the fighting arts will be required to make this effective. However, the martial artists should avoid art-based xenophobia and try to explore other styles/systems – they all have something to offer.

A final point to remember is that, whether trained or untrained, all aggressors are dangerous.

You should be prepared to meet force with force.

In an ideal world, you can talk your way out of it.

In this world, particularly on the streets, face can be lost in this way and most street fighters will not allow this.

Bear these things in mind – Geoff Thompson has many books which address the street-based combat mindset – familiarise yourself with them.

14.0 – Chokes

Does everyone know the difference between a choke and a strangle? No?

Okay....a choke interrupts the air supply to the brain by crushing the throat/neck.

A strangulation interrupts the air supply AND the blood supply to the brain by applying controlled pressure.

Strangulation is by far the faster of the two to incapacitate a would-be assailant.

For clarity, I will call all that I am about to describe as chokes or Shime Waza – choking techniques.

There are six basic chokes we will briefly talk about:

Nami Juji Jime – normal cross choke
Hadaka Jime – naked strangle
Kata Juji Jime – single cross choke
Okuri Eri Jime – sliding lapel choke
Gyaku Juji Jime – reverse cross choke
Kataha Jime – single edge choke

These 'basic' chokes will equip the martial artist with skills to deal with many different violent situations. However, you will need to understand the principles of the techniques to understand the timing and application of the techniques.

Obviously, you cannot just grab your assailant by the throat and expect him/her to wait while you choke them out.

The danger in all chokes is that, if their application timing is mis-judged, your two primary weapons (fists) are tied up and you are vulnerable to attack.

In reality, if you end up grappling and, for some reason, end up underneath your assailant, then Nami Juji Jime could be used.

This is one basic example, see overleaf for more:

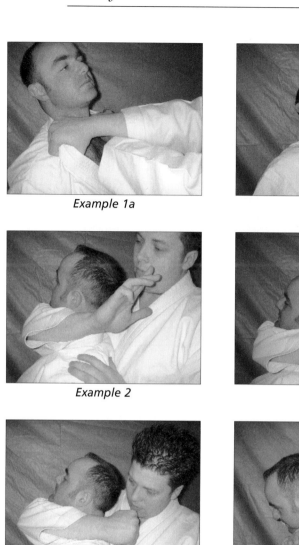
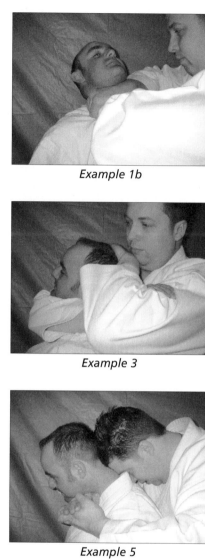

Example 1a

Example 1b

Example 2

Example 3

Example 4

Example 5

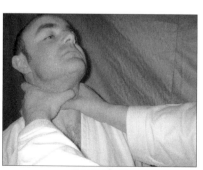
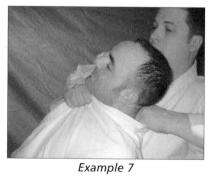

Example 6

Example 7

We will cover these in more detail, and provide counters, within our next book – it'll be worth the wait!

I would like to offer words of caution to those of you who are considering using Shime Waza in your curriculum.

If these techniques are applied incorrectly, a risk of serious injury is apparent.

This could be as severe as the inner walls of the trachea collapsing during the application of a choke and then not re-opening after the technique is removed.

This will almost certainly result in death, even in a Dojo environment.

If the inner walls of the trachea become ruptured, your opponent may drown to death on their own blood.

In a 'live' situation (street combat), with tensions running high and adrenaline pumping, you may apply FAR more pressure than was your intention, resulting in severe injury.

Regardless of the reason, you will be liable for litigation.

Judicious use is strongly recommended.

15.0 – Stances

- What are stances for?
- To look good?
- To improve balance?
- To improve posture?
- Expression of style differences?

No, no, no and no.

In classical interpretation, all of these maybe true – in Jutsu application of Kata, none of them are.

Stances, in Kata, are fluid – we move through stances to achieve the level of power and/or control we desire.

Stances also balance the distribution of body mass to achieve maximum effect in technique delivery.

Coming back to fluidity for a moment – you may know this as Tachi Sabaki or stance movement – one of the most important aspects of combat is 'stance transition'.

A good example of Tachi Sabaki is the following sequence:

Renoji Dachi (V Stance) flowing into Shiko Dachi (Square Stance) flowing into Kokutsu Dachi (Back Stance) flowing into Zenkutsu Dachi (Long Stance).

None of these stances are 'taken', they are merely passed through in the generation of power for the technique you are delivering.

In Renoji Dachi, the body language message is passive.

We tend to adopt Musubi Dachi at 45 degrees when we 'cower'.

This is a good solid stance to deliver hand-strike techniques and from which Tachi Sabaki can be readily commenced.

Here are some common stance examples:

Yoi Dachi

Musubi Dachi

Kiba Dachi

Nekoashi Dachi

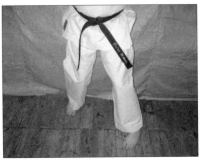

Sanchin Dachi

Moto Dachi

Zenkutsu Dachi

Mae Kosa Dachi

Ushiro Kosa Dachi

Kokutsu Dachi

Naihanchi Dachi

16.0 – Closing comments

You may not yet have noticed how many of the things within this book are triplicate.

No, I don't mean we've copied them three times – I mean a lot of things occur and exist on three levels – let me explain:

- Do – Soft – Way
- Jitsu – Stylised – Art
- Jutsu – Brutally effective – Science

Triangulation of the arms for power.

The three stages of the reverse punch (see effective punching).

- Kimae – Focus – 1st Level
- Zanshin – Awareness – 2nd Level
- Haragei – Spatial awareness – 3rd Level

- Oyo
- Henka
- Kakushi Waza

What does it mean, I hear you say?

I have no idea. However, I do know this:

All of these things are inter-dependent.

One cannot exist without the other(s).

You cannot get from A to D without going through B and C.

Do without Jitsu and Jutsu is empty and futile.

Jitsu without Do and Jutsu is philosophically denuded.

Jutsu without Do and Jitsu is unrestrained violence.

To be a rounded individual, one must have all three parts of all of the above.

The development of the mind, the character, the moral fibre and the conscience of the individual is equally as important as the development of the physique, stamina, physical ability and skill-sets of the individual.

We, as artists, do not start at Do and progress through Jitsu to Jutsu; neither do we observe the same process in reverse.

Do is Jitsu is Jutsu.

Understand?

Karate, as it was originally created/intended/taught, did not have this division.

It simply is.

To truly understand, therefore, you must be all three, simultaneously, without being aware of the transition (back or forth).

Whilst the awareness of the division remains, so does the division – isn't this known as 'mushin'?

Stop trying to analyse it too deeply and just concentrate on being the best you can be.

In closing, we think that we have probably shown that the true nature of Kata is to be devastatingly effective using minimal effort.

It is NOT about being pretty and looking good.

It is NOT about fighting an entire army, at the same time.

It is NOT a technical dance.

We WILL and DO strike first, so should you if necessary.

The pre-emptive strike must be the preferred course of action once all other attempts at avoidance have failed.

DO NOT WAIT TO BE ATTACKED!

An attack can be interpreted as a verbal, physical or scripted assault pattern – learn to interpret the signs and act accordingly.

We NEVER start defensively and what would be the point of ending defensively?

When we end the confrontation, it is with our opponent neutralised at our feet.

As we have stated throughout the book, PLEASE BE CAREFUL WHEN TRYING THESE TECHNIQUES.

THEY DO WORK AND THEY ARE VERY PAINFUL (AND EVEN FATAL).

We hope you have enjoyed our interpretation of Kata in its most raw form.

In our forthcoming publication, we will be looking at the next three levels of Kata, Bunkai and Jutsu, and also, we will be studying more of the grappling aspects, the Kyusho Waza, the joint manipulation and a deeper study of the 'instant stoppers' – the so-called Ikken Hisatsu – stopping an opponent with one blow – and the death and paralysis techniques that Kata was designed to pass-on.

Many thanks for your support and for buying this book.

If we have helped you, even in some small way, to re-think what you are doing and why, then we have achieved our objective.

Finally, many, many thanks go out to Iain Abernethy, without whom we would have struggled far more than we have in preparing this publication and who inspired and encouraged us to publicise our interpretation of the effective application of Kata.

Iain, you're a star!

Happy training!

Domo Arigato Gozaimashita!

Forthcoming Publications

We will be releasing, in the very near future, the second book in the trilogy.

The book will cover the combat Bunkai of Pinan Sandan, Pinan Yondan and Pinan Godan.

It will also cover more in-depth study of striking, kicking, throwing, groundwork, atemi-jutsu, joint and muscle manipulation, Ikken Hisatsu and the Forbidden Points (Death and Paralysis techniques).

If you thought this one was good, you ain't seen nothing yet!

In the third book of the trilogy, we will be covering the combat bunkai of some very old kata, some white crane and high level stuff such as Higaonna Suparinpei, Higaonna Seiunchin and Aragaki Unsu.

There will also be some surprise sections in the groundbreaker.

Look out for them or write to the publishers at the following address to order an advance copy:

BJR Publishing, PO Box 3887, Tipton DY4 8WP, UK.

Visit www.iainabernethy.com for:

- Information on Applied Martial Arts
- Articles on Kata and their Applications
- Details of all of Iain Abernethy's books, videos and DVDs
- Read a Chapter of all of Iain's books
- Seminar Information
- The Latest News
- Subscribe to the FREE Newsletters

Iain Abernethy has been practising martial arts since childhood. Iain's pragmatic approach to traditional systems of combat have made his books and videos very popular with martial artists from all over the world. Iain regularly writes for the UK's leading martial arts magazines and he is a member of "The Combat Hall of Fame".

DEAD OR ALIVE